ART AND POETRY
SIGHT AND INSIGHT

Judith Coxe

LifeRich
PUBLISHING

LifeRich Publishing is a registered trademark of The Reader's Digest Association, Inc.

LifeRich Publishing books may be ordered through booksellers or by contacting:

LifeRich Publishing
1663 Liberty Drive
Bloomington, IN 47403
www.liferichpublishing.com
1 (888) 238-8637

Because of the dynamic nature of the Internet, any web addresses or links contained in this book may have changed since publication and may no longer be valid. The views expressed in this work are solely those of the author and do not necessarily reflect the views of the publisher, and the publisher hereby disclaims any responsibility for them.

© Getty Images:
1) David Hockney:
Photographer, Michael Childers /
Collection, Corbis Entertainment / via Getty Images
2) Pierre Bonnard:
Photographer, A. Natanson in Villeneuve sur Yonne c. 1892 /
by Apic / Collection, Hulton Archive / via Getty Images

ISBN: 978-1-4897-2481-6 (sc)
ISBN: 978-1-4897-2480-9 (hc)
ISBN: 978-1-4897-2479-3 (e)

Library of Congress Control Number: 2019916412

Print information available on the last page.

LifeRich Publishing rev. date: 06/16/2020

Dedication

Among The Hatchlings

On my desk
I keep a nest.

Will I ever discover
in my collection
of crooked images,
pressed so eagerly together,
a startling cuckoo
of a poem?

To my husband Don,
and my splendid family.

To my poetic partners,
Peter Oyloe & Emile Kemp.

Contents

DRAMATIC
MONOLOGUES

Genie In A Bottle
In 1912, Luigi Boccioni made a silver/bronze sculpture,
15 inches tall, called, "The Development of a Bottle in Space".
Its flayed body runs out across the table top in the museum,
succumbing to entropy, it comes to nothing in the end.

Genie In A Bottle

I am Real.
I am a spirit of the Air,
just as you are of the Earth.
I am a spirit of the Night,
free to vanish
with the fading of the stars.

Offer me
the power of your wish.

Wish for me
that I transcend
this metal skin,
this coffin of bronze,
these alien walls.

Grant this,
and I will offer you hope.

I will free you
from the fading of the light,
from the dwindling of this world

you think you know.

Love Letter From Pierre Bonnard
Artist, Pierre Bonnard 1892

Love Letter From Pierre Bonnard

Immediately after sundown
the dining room is hot and still.
The shadows on the window frame
are rose-pink. After dinner,
you unbutton your dress,
and ease your orange skirt
high up over your thighs.
You lean back
against the violet wall. Suddenly
your glowing face is kissed
with the soft green
of antique bronze.
You turn your eyes away
and we do not speak.

This morning, Marthe,
I set up my easel.

Your dressing table
is an altar decked
in cascades of bridal lace.

I see myself
in the angle
of your mirror.

The frame has
cut away my hands
and feet, and
cropped off my head.

I had painted myself
without the means
to think or feel
without you.

David Hockney Flies To Los Angeles
David Hockney, 1978

David Hockney Flies To Los Angeles

Back home in Bradford,
in dull November,
always tea-time.

The earth's hump
leaps and sinks
with no traces,
the desert
submerges its
secret places.
Chaos crouches,
shuddering
with haunted
dreams,
beneath the freeways
phosphorescent streams.

A martini!
Magenta socks!

Thank God, at last!!

Record The Message

Record The Message

[After the beep...]

Hey, Luke, it's me.
Out golfing? Lucky bastard.
You've called a coupla times.
Sorry, we've been real busy here.
Jeez...three months since you retired...
since you gave us reasons...
Darlene says they let you go.
I didn't know.
Sales results were lousy at year end...
Christ, I didn't see it coming.
Darlene's the one to get it right.
Joe's got your old desk now...
Joe saw her killing a bottle with the CEO
at the Four Seasons just last night.
Darlene only goes for guys with dough,
that's no surprise, but that old bugger,
what a scum, I never thought he'd
dump you, Luke.
You go way back.
How's Ruthie? How're the kids?
Both still in college? Haven't
seen you at the club.
I'll buy you a drink and
we'll catch up, but
not till August, though. We're
going crazy here.
I'll call you one day soon.
We'll fix a day.
So long, ol' Buddy.

The Jungle

The Jungle

Here we are in the jungle.

Oops!

It is a frigid Brooklyn warehouse in January!
They gave me boots, a hat, peculiar underwear.

I huddle in my winter coat among the props.

At dawn, they opened the rattling doors
to a battered jeep, also a load of tree trunks,
and a canopy of branches,
perhaps of some exotic species?
Wait! I think they are plastic!
Here, no hum and squeak of insects,
just the rattle and screech of metallic parts!

Thank God, they have turned on the lights at last.
I will start to sweat and please the surly art director.

Here is my Valentino dress at last!

"Sexy is what we need!
Stretch out, writhe a bit, do sultry.
Adrian, move those lights
to cast her face into deep shadow.
Highlight the cleavage!"

I imagine ladies in my Valentino
mingling at the Plaza Hotel,
sniffing out the hottest celebrities.

"Fantastic, darling! Just what I had in mind."

St Mary's, Virgin Gorda
(From the memorial service for Hazel.)

St Mary's, Virgin Gorda

(IN MEMORY OF HAZEL)

In the churchyard
above the sea,
a wall of boulders
shields a new grave
from the insolence
of goats.

The gravestone is tiled
with border tiles,
tiles with wreaths
and swags,
tiles painted with
flowers from
exotic English gardens,
with blue roses,
with violets,
and daisies.

A scarlet insect,
his vermilion wings
folded along his back,
has clambered
up a tall stem
tossing
in the sea wind,

anticipating Paradise?

The Honeyman

The Honeyman

I say, everything here
she be ruled by the moon.
When the moon is gone,
the bees they work for me.
They quiet on their backs
when I clean the hive.
Not a bite,
not one.

But when the new moon come,
they bite right through
the shirt, the gloves.

Why do I stay
when the new moon come?
What cost a first class ticket to Australia?

See my three shelves there,
lined with little jars from everywhere,
a hundred honeys packed in a wooden comb.
Honey of Singapore or Fiji
or Brisbane tastes strange.

My wife she stay
and sing in church
Let the Heaven Shine on Me.

But I say,
everything here
she be ruled by the moon.

New moon, cool season,
come,
taste the finest hibiscus honey.

Snow White And Her Stepmother

Snow White And Her Stepmother

Before I ran away
you only cared
for your own beauty.

Your magic mirror
never lies to you,
whatever you may wish.

You came at last hiding in
a ragged cloak, but I saw you in
the gleam of doorknobs.

You offered shining
poisoned apples, but I
knew the face reflected there.

But now I am coffined
in a tomb of glittering glass.
How long have I been here?

I still covet the pretty poisoned apples
you offered me, urging me to choose.
Dare I wish that you will come again?

*I hear the thud and jingle
of approaching horses.*

Who might this be coming
to lift the glass,
to kiss my frozen cheek?

Dzoonokwa's Basket
In the folk tales of the Pacific Northwest, Dzoonokwa is the
wild woman of the woods who carries off children to eat.

Dzoonokwa's Basket

Here I was a child;
a child who leaped over clotted tangles
of kelp and bladder wrack,
and chased a bulky raven
down the streaming beach.

I am old and hungry now.
I have seen the gray Pacific roll whole trees,
scoured to bones, to the green edge of the forest.
With my empty basket on my knees,
I wait here,
concealed under the
claw of this bare root.

In fog,
in silence,
the gaping mouth
of my basket
trembles and creaks.

I sense
a child walking
out of the mist,
pressing breath from the stones
with faint footfalls.

Wandered Off

Wandered Off

She has never
wandered off before,

a city cat, albino,
used to carpet,
out of place among
starved pines
and olive water.

I bring him a lap robe
against the sharp wind,
and find him a patch of sun
at the end of the deck.

She was sitting on his lap.

He must have nodded off,
didn't feel her go.
He never leaves the cottage deck
now that he is sick again.

Why has she wandered off?
Why now,
to grieve him so?

The lake is furred and gray,
twitching like a cat
flexing its claws.

No chairs yet on the dock
this early in the season, so
I sit alone in the tethered boat.

On The Labrador
An Innu mummer.

On The Labrador
(The Grandmother)

Here on the Labrador,
in summer
when I was a child,
my grandfather limbed
out white ends,
and sweet pine smoke
rose from dry wood.
From the cold pit
I brought caribou meat
to the fire.

We feasted all night
with the Merry Dancers
flickering in the sky.

Then the Innu learned from
watching their Elders.

What can my grandchildren
still learn from me now?
They scatter like
frightened caribou
among trees
too thin for cover.
My cheeks are wet with tears.
We have lost our season,
and here is winter again.

On The Labrador, Long Home
(The Grandson)

On The Labrador, Long Home
(The Grandson)

True caribou heart,
my lost little brother,
calling to me amid
the groans of winter trees!

Your cheeks caught fire

when the candle
toppled in our
closed house,

when the burning gasoline
chased down your throat,
when I ran away.

Your lost heart
has come back for me!

Blue fire, radiant and loving,
comes to guide me
to where you are lost and alone.

You loosen the cover
of your grave,
and the wind lifts it,
beckoning me to follow you.

We cry together.
The red painted heart
I made for you
bleeds in the fallen snow.

THROUGH AN ARTIST'S EYE

My Tropic Muse?

My Tropic Muse?

Are you my tardy Muse at last?
A buxom bee, blundering
about the bougainvillea?

I'd settle for a red hibiscus as my Muse
if she had a big fat smooch,
right now, for me alone.

Night Wall

Night Wall

At sundown,
from rocky field,
from thorn and cactus,
to the soft dust of the road,
the cattle came.

Each sound is distinct.
The muffled thump of hooves,
the click of small raindrops
on dry leaves,
oboe of a mourning dove.

The wall of the schoolyard
is darker than the night sky
punctured with stars.
The beam of our flashlight
is a dim ring sliding
in and out of footprints.

By day,
the wooden wall had
painted waves,
and fish,
and palm trees
under the yellow sun.
At the top of the fence
in red letters it read

"SHINE ON, HEART-LIGHT".

By night,
the black wall silently breathes
the accumulated heat of the afternoon.
The velvet herd merges with the night wall,
a heavy head turning,
a gleam from a dark eye.

All warmth and rich breath,
herd and wall,
exhaling together.

Blue On The Brush
Where's the blue?

Blue On The Brush

Hot-lick blue
trumpets the tropic sky.

Sweet Cerulean,
Meissen blue,
china blue,
blue shards
knifing
between boulders.

Ultramarine,
like tarnished ink,
scores the open sea
with upstart waves.

On the golden beach
a white cat
tumbles into shadow
and emerges
violet-blue.

Tropic Noon

Tropic Noon

Feral cats
mewl unintelligibly
like far-off children.

A calico cat stalks soundlessly
among lobed shadows of sea-grape.

A small plane pours its
shadow over sun-burned rocks.

The cat springs away, mouth agape.

Terns
Bay occupied by terns.

Terns

Out in the bay,
seven white terns
face the rising sun,
each blazing feather
rimmed with gold.

A motionless
honor guard
in single file
stands on a spine of rock.

A shadow passes,
and their fiery white
is now dull ash in
a cinder sea.

The Rock Café and Sports Bar, The Valley, Virgin Gorda

The Rock Cafe And Sports Bar,
The Valley, Virgin Gorda

Twenty years ago,
this roundabout
where dirt roads meet,
contained the public well.

Here chestnut cattle with gentle eyes
shifted slowly from the concrete trough
to the shade of a stunted tree.
In the hot season when
the well was dry,
they whimpered
and stamped the ground
all night.

Now the Rock Cafe and Sports Bar
stands at this crossroads.
Inside, the light is dim
as in deep water, and the air is cool.
Pool balls like multi-colored fish
slip over reefs of green baize;
Tankards of beer flash back
the light of seven giant screens
as the thirsty Valley drinks in
the outside world.

Sunset, Virgin Gorda

Sunset, Virgin Gorda

On his evening rounds,
patrolling the sea-grape hedge,
the calico cat,
blue in shadow,
marks out his territory.

He pirouettes, pauses, sprays,
unsheathes his claws,
stretches his white leg
into the last of the sunlight.

Pelicans

Pelicans

Pelicans have convened
on the dark reef
that runs out along the bay.

So many
untidy parcels of
soggy flotsam!

One by one they
slip away to skim
their shabby hats
over the furrowed sea,

and soar.

Lightening raids,
wings tucked for speed!

Or a solo sortie

with a slow descent,

a single grubby
parachute,
wafts uncertainly
before the final twist,

the gulp and the nod.

Marking Time

Marking Time

Rain vanishes
in blinding storms,

rain seeps into earth,
into ditch and stream,

rain hisses and spits,
chasing tide
across a shining flat.

Pock, pock,
pock, pock,
pock, pock,
pucker and squeeze,
as the moon snail
sucks and glides
on his fleshy foot.

Youth is so beautiful,
yet it flees!
People who want to be happy
should be happy:
there's no certainty in the future.

Quant' e bella giovanezza
che si fugge tuttavia
Chi vuol esser lieto, sia
di doman non c'e certezza.

Lorenzo de Medici, Song for Bacchus

Train To Firenze

The station stop at Montecantini;

on the opposite platform
young girls with knapsacks
are bound for Viareggio.
In capri pants and halter tops,
they wave smooth hands,
with painted nails
and cigarettes.

Beautiful boys
in leather jackets
huddle together,
half turned away.

But I am bound for Firenze.

Too soon,
Montecantini
slides past the windows;
we pass a cemetery
like a frescoed town.
Tombs of pink brick
frame an empty piazza.
White crosses spring
from bare pavement.

Too soon,
a hill topped with towers
darkens under a passing cloud.
The carriage slides into
a tunnel, reeking of
burning tar.

Mirror

Mirror

I see myself,
mirrored in a glassy pond,
my face in shadow,
brown and green,
crowned by random
leaves which
spin languidly
in the pond's gentle
downstream tug.
My mind flexes
among glittering
dust motes and
shifting spiders.
For a moment,
I dream alone
among the water lilies.

The Beach At Point-No-Point, Vancouver Island

A landscape must be focused like a camera,
for an all inclusive depth of field
or selective close-up.

My choice of vantage point
is among the watchful birds
who pace the crew-cut cliff
above the beach.

We begin in distance,
blurred white,
mist along the horizon,
muffs of low cloud
cushioning the far peaks
of the Olympic peninsula.

Then, up close, we examine
a throng of blackberries
and wild roses,
sunshades of cow parsley,
plumes of ostrich fern,
torches of beach lupine.

Edges of the view
now flow to the core,
to a single image of
deep grooves in
the tidal flats,
gray and glittering with ripples,
singing in a shimmer of strings.

Nuance and timbre are also
common to music and landscape!

Bleached tree trunks
are stacked like sewer pipes,
bristling like cannon
in a black rampart of blistered rock.
Cello solo and then a roll of drums.

Like a musical composition
a landscape cannot
be comprehended all at once,
but must be compounded
like the vision of a grasshopper,
from a mosaic of separate moments.

In the sea there is
a mosaic among the waves
with their flux and flow.
White curls of foam,
fuzzy lines of chalk
on gray board,
steam where the cold sea
wipes the sand.

Landscape offers a poet a way
of looking without a single destination.

The shadow of a bird
flickers across the beach,
and is lost again,

Whiffen Spit,
Vancouver Island

Whiffen Spit,
Vancouver Island

The spit sprawls
in a long curve
like a flattened sail.

Clumps of dog roses,
stunted tufts of purple vetch,
and saffron broom,
all bend attentively,

dry ears pressed to stone.

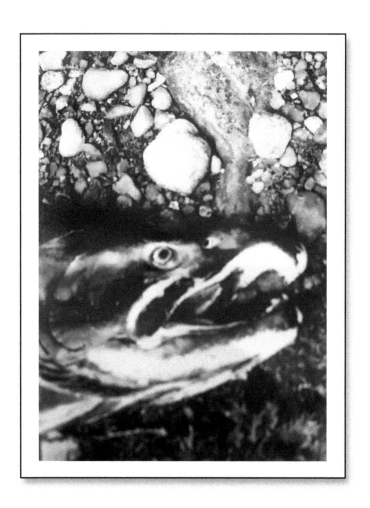

On The Goldstream River,
Vancouver Island

On The Goldstream River, Vancouver Island

The Dipper wades upstream,
retracing no history,
making no judgments.

He slips
below the surface,
his needle beak
stripping bare
the bones
of salmon.

Whatever the
the careless river
leaves behind
will presently
be his.

To The Tree-Line

To The Tree-Line

Let us refuse everything that
might hoist us to breathless everlasting
pinnacles without flowers.
        Fernando Pessoa

We hoist our heavy packs,
        breathe deeply, heads bent,
        hike steadily higher.

On a windless trail,
        through old burn-out, young birch trees
        toss sunlight from trunk to trunk.

A still lake is paved with gold,
        stained emerald green by
        sunlit slabs of buried shale.

Just below the summit, now strewn with toppled trunks,
        an avalanche has opened a wound
        across the saddle between the peaks.

Here the soil is spare. The air is thin. The snow
        has not melted by cool July. Green shoots
        shiver as if a spirit walked the grass.

Here on the pinnacle, golden glacier lilies bow,
        swinging their heads like gilded censers,
        blessing a hapless world.

Rite of Spring

Rite Of Spring

There is something
vegetable
about the imagination,
probing for
holes and weak spots
where the mind can root
and sprout.

When the oak tree
buds antlers
of new green,
and the apple tree
spreads long fingers
trembling with bells,
ambition plants the world
in a nursery bed.

I must have a child
to love forever.

Ramsey Canyon, Arizona

Ramsey Canyon, Arizona

On my vacation windowsill,
sit hinged daguerreotypes
cased in tooled leather.

The photos show a foreign couple,
a bearded man in a formal suit,
a woman stiffly corseted in black.
Both have wary, frozen faces,
fixed for the camera's flash.

Outside the window
this morning early, came
a flock of wild turkeys,
dowdy, dun-colored,
foraging together,
under the stunted oaks.
They suffered a peacock
to creep among them,
keeping his distance,
head down, dragging
his furled magnificence
through the dusty scrub.

Where did they come from,
these refugees, and this
frightened peacock?
Why did they come here,
to this obstinate landscape
of ferocious cutlery
and eleven kinds of rattlesnake?

Bedroom in Maine

Bedroom In Maine

The gabled room brims
with light from the sea,
a room of possibilities,
of shadows clasping
and letting go.

Once upon a time,
I opened every tube
in my new paint box, and
painted a rose tree
on the wall.

It still floats
where I painted it
so long ago,
on the wall
by the door,
where the stair turns.

Gertrude Stein Had
A Voice Like A Beefsteak

Gertrude Stein Had
A Voice Like A Beefsteak

Rough smells of
sweat and garlic,
Turkish cigarettes,
cut freesias,
and *moules marinières.*

She shifts her corseted body
in its slither of dull crepe.
One hooded eye is fixed;
the other swings, unhinged.

Above the screeching
of caged birds,

that beefsteak voice.

Mirror, Mirror

Mirror, Mirror

Here you are,
meeting my eyes.

Surely I have seen
your face before!

Together we must once
have wakened to the
drumming of hammers,
and danced on the
Seven Mountains.

I know I would
know for sure,
if only
I could remember.

Archaeopteryx

In *The Science Times*,
today is a drawing,
half dinosaur,
half bird.

The artist has drawn him
with his neck knotted,
his eyes popping,
his bulky drumsticks thrusting
against the ground,
straining to fly.

He makes him look like
a plucked chicken
fleeing the oven.

Would I hear
the scraping of
bone against bone,
the rasp of breath,
or see the crust
of cold flesh
sprouting alarm?

Oh, if I could,

I would cradle him
in down,
soft as pollen
clinging to the
antlers of lilies.

I would costume him
with a radiant tail,
wise with a thousand eyes,
and gird him with wings

to sweep
a loving shadow
over all the world!

The Red Fox

The Red Fox

Bird alarm sprays
from the maple bush.

I see the red fox
streaming flat out
across the radiant field.

He dances on a cat's cradle,
bending and swaying
on his rock-a-bye bridge.

My stubborn mouth
is full of pebbles,
struggling to speak.

End Of Winter

End Of Winter

The lake sleeps
like a snake,
cold-blooded,
tarnished green.

One red-cold sunrise
warms its sluggish blood.
It begins to roll
in languorous coils
over the breakwater.

Sedona, Arizona

Sedona, Arizona

At the base
of the red mesa
the Sinagua people
cower in rooms piled high,
huddle like starving children,
who press against
a mother with a
swollen belly
full of blood.

Stunted old men
climb crumbling ladders
to paint the signs
they need to live;
a scorpion with a curled tail,
a tower with many rooms,
a rippling snake,
a cleft circle, and
a man playing a flute.

Over their heads a raven
claps his black wings,
and flows into the rock.

Under a thorn tree,
whose black berries
explode like dead stars,
a rabbit with a single eye,
freezes her long ears
against her stony back.

Above the parched sand,
only her mouth moves.

Holland

Holland

It's only Holland,
the natives say ruefully.

What do they mean to say?

The people of the Netherlands
are the tallest in Europe.

They do admit this!

We see them through
large front windows,
candidly eating and talking,
climbing their corkscrew stairs,
too tall for their doll-houses,
but with nothing at all to hide.

London Light

London Light

Fond Man, the vision of a moment made,
Dream of a dream, and shadow of a shade.
        Milton, Paradise Lost.

In the Victoria and Albert,
the librarian passes me
a pair of white gloves,
and a wooden box labeled
SAMUEL PALMER
Shoreham Period
1820-1835.

My white gloves
lift out a pencil drawing
on virgin paper
white, immaculate,
of a pastoral landscape,
of scattered woods, a valley,
and the pale heights beyond.

But it is Samuel Palmer
who joins me here
in this hushed room,
washed with the
silvery light of London.

He draws his image of
Ancient England.
It is a Paradise
where shepherds piped,
and clouds dropped fatness.
Every material thing he draws
is given a second life, reborn.

He pulls back the veil of Heaven,
the curtain before eternity.

Goodbye

Goodbye

In chronic care
in Miami
my father
is pinioned
to a gurney.

An old bird
right enough,
his brain
worn out,
an unmanned post,
a dusty key,
no message
to be sent
by living will.

A shaking throat,
a speaking eye,
calling my name.

Bob Dylan

Bob Dylan

In 2009, in New Jersey,
police encountered a man staring
into dark and empty windows.
He said he was Bob Dylan.

Hard driving rain confines you
as you pace and pace.
You are a hooded wanderer,
dancing in tiny circles,
a disheveled old man
staring into the windows
of vacant houses.

You are drumming words,
from the blues
and the news.

Words which howl
and growl,
as you beat your fists
on the black ground.

Mrs. Noah

Mrs. Noah

We are an old pair,
Noah and I, together
since long and ever ago.

But for every old shoe,
they say,
there is an old sock.
We are a pair still
even if we are in for
a long streak of misery.

So, look spry, Noah,
here comes another squall!
It's raining
cats and dogs again,
claws down.

No More Light
(from a family album)

No More Light

When I was four,
my father and I
paddled close to the
shore of an island
in Lake Simcoe.
We looked down into
green luminous depths,
flooded with brilliant sunlight.
We saw pale furred rocks
and shells far below.
"Dive down and
bring me a shell," he said.
"I have 50 cents for you!"

I dove into the light.

Having outlived
his life expectancy
by several months,
my father was
sent to me to die.
It was July and the lawn
was a vivid green,
pulsating with
dappled shadow.
I set up chairs, and
he walked out with me,
His hand shielding his eyes, he said,
"I think I have had
enough light in my life."
I helped him inside to his bed.
There I pulled the golden blind
to protect him from the light.

SIGHT AND INSIGHT

No Poem Here?

NOTES FOR SMUGGLER'S COVE, TORTOLA, B.V.I.

*Seamus Heaney, "How perilous it is not
to love the life we are shown."*

The green and white boat, lying on its side,
was here twenty years ago.
Now it is only a few weathered planks
half buried in the sand.

So few changes here,
the washings of the tide,
whorls in the sand on the sea bottom,
always subtly different,
always the same.

At the Smuggler's Cove Bar,
a skewed sign reads OPEN,
propped against a grimy ashtray,
on a card with faded ink.

HONOUR BAR,
DRINKS IN THE
WHITE FRIDGE.

It seems to have been undisturbed for years.
The bar is decorated with flotsam from the beach,
everything saved, and
honored for surviving.
Sea fans in a basket,
palm fronds nailed to the rafters,
everything brown and dry.
Sand has drifted in to cover the floor.

Behind the Bar,
are three green glass
demijohns, dull as sea glass,
cracked and filmed with dust.
On a table, is a tattered book,
The Hazards of Navigation.

On the bar, an old color photo,
faded to blue,
shows a barely recognizable
Queen Elizabeth,
much younger than she is today.

In the photo she leans from the window
of a white Lincoln Continental.

And there it is,
the Lincoln Continental,
rusted at the seams.

Driven under the open bar,
with a shattered windshield,
to be an object of admiration.

The owner, an old man
in a solar topee,
has eyes still young and sharp.

Green rollers smack a yellow beach.
The white sea floor is veined with gold.
Minnows of light herd together.

Rocks

Rocks

In the beginning there were words,
precise, fine-tuned, concrete words,
some sharp as hailstones,
as self-contained
as rocks on an icy shore.

But other words are other rocks,
allusive,
metaphoric,
shape changers,
some rough,
some smooth,
some shiny,
some brilliantly theatrical
when under water.

A word can even be a rock
like an uncut diamond,
its brilliance
turned inward.
Its meaning is
too complex
to reveal
its intimate self
in a single encounter.

Shall I duck and cover?

Optimism is best in the morning,
not so easy after lunch.
I will sit on the rocky shore
and watch the sun go down.

Inspiration
(from a family album)

Inspiration

Inspiration,
without a compass,
folds awareness in upon itself.
It is a singing river
surging to an unknown sea.
There are no rules
to guide its music.

Inspiration
spins among the stars
to the rhythmic pounding
of the heart.

GATHERING
ROSEBUDS!

Gathering Rosebuds!

My garden plot seems quite a lot
like Sodom and Gomorrah.
My roses, ever hot to trot,
twine, splice and clamber, all besot!

Sexy Rexy, with *Betty Prior,*
propagates freely, will never tire.
Double Delight is so delectable,
Handel's tastes are all bisexual.

Don Juan woos with winking eye,
that wanton widow, *Constance Spry.*
Though she is cankered, woody, old,
he's lusting for her *Sutter's Gold.*

Brandy twists with madness lunar,
girdling his graft with *Cecile Brunner.*
Elizabeth Taylor, still a starlet
beats her lover 'til *Paul's Scarlet.*

Eye Paint, *French Lace*, and sweet undress
enhance the charms of *Dainty Bess*,
seducing *Sonia*, louche and tarty
at *Madame Hardy's Garden Party*.

No scourge of vice, our *Rambling Rector*,
rumored an S and M director.
With canes he thwacks the tempting tush-ke
of nymphomaniac *Frau Karl Drushke*.

My garden plot seems quite a lot
like Sodom and Gomorrah.
Rosaceae think no virtuous thought,
don't read the Bible, need the Torah.
They have no call for ethics text;
they never fret they're oversexed.
No scandal here; let gossip cease.
We'll leave them all to lust in *Peace*.